A CORE COLLECTION IN PRESERVATION

Compiled by Lisa L. Fox

for the Education Committee of the Preservation of Library Materials Section, Resources and Technical Services Division, American Library Association

Chicago: Resources and Technical Services Division
American Library Association 1988

Cover designed by Deb Doering

Text supplied on disk by the author
and composed by Stuart Whitwell
in Palatino, output to a
laser printer

Printed on 50-pound Glatfelter,
a pH-neutral stock, and bound
in 10-point Carolina cover
stock by Versa Press, Inc.
∞

Library of Congress Cataloging-in-Publication Data

Fox, Lisa L.
    A core collection in preservation / Lisa L. Fox for the Education
Committee, Preservation of Library Materials Section.
        p. cm.
    ISBN 0-8389-7224-1 (pbk.) : $5.00
    1. Books—Conservation and restoration—Bibliography. 2. Library
materials—Conservation and restoration—Bibliography. 3. Archival
materials—Conservation and restoration—Bibliography. I. American
Library Association. Preservation of Library Materials Section.
Education Committee. II. Title.
Z701.F69 1988
016.0257—dc19   88-12102
                                                              CIP

CONTENTS

Titles in this bibliography are arranged in the following areas:

A CORE COLLECTION IN PRESERVATION

Compiled by Lisa L. Fox
for the Preservation of Library Materials Section,
ALA Resources & Technical Services Division
(February 1988)

"A Core Collection in Preservation" lists and annotates those books, reports, periodicals, and major articles that are likely to be most useful in preservation planning and administration. Titles have been included to cover the entire spectrum of library and archival preservation and to provide a working resource for administrators, librarians, archivists, curators, conservators, and others working to preserve our documentary heritage. This bibliography is not exhaustive, but includes those publications which, after critical review by members of the PLMS Education Committee, have been judged accurate, useful, and especially significant.

The knowledge base of the preservation field is growing rapidly, so even relatively recent publications may include some information that is no longer fully accurate. Therefore, users of this bibliography are encouraged to read these works critically and to apply them conservatively. Highly technical works and those in non-English languages have been excluded.

Acquisition information follows each annotation. Most items were in print at the time of inclusion in this bibliography, but a few seminal works that are out of print have been included in hopes that they can be borrowed through interlibrary loan networks. Sources and prices were accurate as of the time of inclusion. Some prices include shipping, and others do not; check with the publisher before ordering.

I. GENERAL WORKS & BIBLIOGRAPHIES

American Association for State and Local History. *Technical Leaflet Series.*

Over 100 short leaflets with sound, practical guidance for the small library, archive, museum, and historical society. Preservation topics covered include exhibitions, basic care and handling, photographs, and artifacts.

AASLH Order/Billing Dept., 172 Second Ave. North, Suite 102, Nashville, TN 37201 (615-255-2971). $2.00 per leaflet.

Atkinson, Ross W. "Selection for Preservation: A Materialistic Approach." *Library Resources & Technical Services* 30: 341-53 (Oct./Dec. 1986).

Proposes a strategy for selecting materials to be preserved and for choosing the appropriate means to preservation, focusing especially on microfilming. While controversial, the essay suggests an approach to rationalizing the selection process.

Boyd, Jane, and Don Etherington. *Preparation of Archival Copies of Theses and Dissertations.* Chicago: ALA, 1986. 15 p.

Detailed instructions, including guidelines on paper quality, illustrations, photographs, oversized pages, duplication, sound recordings, and binding.

ALA, 50 East Huron St., Chicago, IL 60611 (800-545-2433). $3.95, plus shipping.

Child, Margaret S. "Further Thoughts on 'Selection for Preservation: A Materialistic Approach.'" *Library Resources & Technical Services* 30: 354-62 (Oct./Dec. 1986).

Outlines criteria for preservation selection in the context of a nationally coordinated strategy, and discusses the importance of developing selection strategies for archival, as well as library materials.

Cunha, George M., and Dorothy G. Cunha. *Conservation of Library Materials: A Manual and Bibliography on the Care, Repair and Restoration of Library Materials.* 2 vols. 2nd ed. Metuchen, NJ: Scarecrow Press, 1971-72. Vol. 2, 414 p.

Volume 2 is a comprehensive bibliography on book and paper preservation, arranged by subject, with an author index.

Scarecrow Press, 52 Liberty St., Box 4167, Metuchen, NJ 08440 (201-548-8600). $27.50 each, set $45; plus shipping.

-----. *Library and Archives Conservation: 1980s and Beyond.* 2 vols. Metuchen, NJ: Scarecrow Press, 1983. Vol. 2, 415 p.

Bibliography (vol. 2) emphasizes the previous ten years; designed for use in conjunction with their earlier work (cited above).

Scarecrow Press, 52 Liberty St., Box 4167, Metuchen, NJ 08840 (201-548-8600). Vol. 1, $18; vol. 2, $32.50; set, $42.50; plus shipping.

1

Darling, Pamela W., and Wesley Boomgaarden, compilers. *Preservation Planning Program: Resource Notebook.* Expanded 1987 edition. Washington: ARL Office of Management Studies, 1987. 675 pages.

Excellent source of bibliographies, background and technical readings, and important ephemeral materials useful in areas of library preservation planning and implementation. Developed for use with Darling's *Manual* (see section VIII).

ARL/OMS, 1527 New Hampshire Ave. NW, Washington, DC 20036 (202-232-8656). $35. Prepayment required.

Morrow, Carolyn Clark, with Gay Walker. *The Preservation Challenge: A Guide to Conserving Library Materials.* White Plains, NY: Knowledge Industry Publications, 1983. 231 p.

Excellent overview of preservation information, with useful guidance on administrative concerns (policy establishment, staffing, budgeting, etc.).

G. K. Hall, 70 Lincoln St., Boston, MA 02111 (617-423-3990). $34.50 hardcover, $27.50 soft.

National Association of Government Archives and Records Administrators. *Preservation Needs in State Archives.* Albany, NY: NAGARA, 1986. 72 p.

The result of an in-depth study of preservation needs and capabilities in state archives, this document presents findings on current activities, describes the most pressing needs, and outlines steps to be taken to develop a coordinated, effective program among government archives.

NAGARA, c/o New York State Archives, Room 10A75, Cultural Education Center, Albany, NY 12230. Free.

Preservation of Library Materials. IFLA Publications 40/41. 2 vols. Edited by Merrily Smith. Munich: K. G. Saur Verlag, 1987. 305 p.

Proceedings of a conference held at the National Library of Austria, 7-10 April 1986, by the Conference of Directors of National Libraries, including 39 speakers from 17 countries. Volume 1 focuses on theoretical/conceptual topics, including policy, planning, cooperation, and emerging technologies. Volume 2 includes technical presentations on policy and training, reproduction, storage and handling, treatment, and environment. Provides an international perspective on needs, priorities, and solutions. Essays in English, with French and German summaries.

K. G. Saur, 175 5th Ave., New York, NY 10010 (212-982-1302). $70.

Ritzenthaler, Mary Lynn. *Archives and Manuscripts: Conservation.* SAA Basic Manual Series. Chicago: Society of American Archivists, 1983. 151 p.

A comprehensive guide to the field of archival preservation.

SAA, 600 South Federal St., Suite 504, Chicago, IL 60605 (312-922-0140). $15, $11 members, plus shipping.

Slow Fires: On the Preservation of the Human Record. Santa Monica, CA: American Film Foundation, 1987. Color. 30- and 60-min. versions in 16mm, VHS, or 3/4" cassette formats.

Describes the loss of the world's intellectual heritage through the deterioration of library and archival materials, focusing on brittle paper. Also discusses reformatting options (particularly microfilming), selection for preservation, disasters, and the need for increased use of alkaline paper. Useful for staff education, and especially good for public and academic programs.

American Film Foundation, Box 2000, Santa Monica, CA 90406 (213-459-2116 or 213-394-5689). In VHS format: $39.50 for 30-min., $59.50 for 60-min. version. 3/4" cassette: $105 for 30-min., $145 for 60-min. version. 16mm film format: $550 for 30-min., $750 for 60-min. version. Plus $10 shipping. Rentals also available.

Swartzburg, Susan G. *Preserving Library Materials: A Manual.* Metuchen, NJ: Scarecrow Press, 1980. 282 p.

A basic guide to help librarians, especially those with smaller collections, analyze needs and develop collection maintenance programs.

Scarecrow Press, 52 Liberty St., Box 4167, Metuchen, NJ 08840 (201-548-8600). $17.50, plus shipping.

SEE ALSO: V. Research Libraries Group; VI. Swartzburg

II. PAPER & ENVIRONMENT

American National Standards Institute. *American National Standard for Information Sciences: Permanence of Paper for Printed Library Materials.* ANS Z39.48-1984. New York: ANSI, 1985. 8 p.

Establishes the criteria for permanence of uncoated paper, covering specifications for pH, alkaline reserve, freedom from groundwood, folding endurance, and resistance to tears.

ANSI Sales Dept., 1430 Broadway, New York, NY 10018 (212-354-3300). $5, plus $2 shipping. Prepayment required.

Banks, Paul N. "Preservation of Library Materials." *Encyclopedia of Library and Information Science.* Vol. 23, pp. 180-222.

Good overview of the causes of deterioration and of preservation methods, concentrating on the key role played by environmental conditions in the repository.

Clapp, Verner W. "The Story of Permanent/Durable Paper, 1115-1970," in *Scholarly Publishing* 2: 107-24, 229-45, 353-67 (Jan., April, July 1971). Also published separately as Supplement 3 of *Restaurator*, Copenhagen: Munksgaard, 1972; 51 p.

History of developments in paper-making which gave rise to the problem of deterioration in modern paper, with account of Barrow's efforts to develop a permanent/durable paper. Essential reading.

Munksgaard International Publishers, Nørre Søgade, P. O. Box 2148, DK-1016 Copenhagen K, Denmark.

Hollinger, William. "The Chemical Structure and Acid Deterioration of Paper." *Library Hi Tech* 1: 51-57 (Spring 1984).

A thorough discussion of the effects of acid on paper. Technical, but comprehensible (with effort) by the non-scientist.

Lafontaine, R. H. *Recommended Environmental Monitors for Museums, Archives and Art Galleries.* Technical Bulletin 3. Ottawa: Canadian Conservation Institute, 1980. 22 p.

Good discussion of monitoring equipment for measuring relative humidity, temperature, lighting levels, and air pollution. Some sections now slightly dated, as new instruments have become available; but a good introduction.

Canadian Conservation Institute, 1030 Innes Road, Ottawa, Canada K1A 0M8 (613-998-3721). Free. Also reproduced in Darling and Boomgaarden (cited in section I).

Lafontaine, Raymond H., and Patricia A. Wood. *Fluorescent Lamps.* Technical Bulletin 7. Ottawa: Canadian Conservation Institute, 1980. 14 p.

Explains the operation and visual characteristics of fluorescent lamps, with emphasis on ultraviolet emission levels and visual appropriateness of various types of lamps.

Canadian Conservation Institute, 1030 Innes Road, Ottawa, Canada K1A 0M8 (613-998-3721). Free. Also reproduced in Darling and Boomgaarden (cited in section I).

Macleod, K. J. *Relative Humidity: Its Importance, Measurement and Control in Museums.* Technical Bulletin 1. Ottawa: Canadian Conservation Institute, 1975, reprinted 1978. 14 p.

Excellent discussion of relative humidity, including recommended levels, ways of measurement, and methods for control.

Canadian Conservation Institute, 1030 Innes Road, Ottawa, Canada K1A 0M8 (613-998-3721). Free. Also reproduced in Darling and Boomgaarden (cited in section I).

Metcalf, Keyes D. *Planning Academic and Research Library Buildings.* 2nd ed. by Philip D. Leighton and David C. Weber. Chicago: ALA, 1986. 630 p.

Comprehensive guide to building design, with considerable attention to preservation considerations.

ALA, 50 East Huron St., Chicago, IL 60611 (800-545-2433). $60, plus shipping.

Story, Keith O. *Approaches to Pest Management in Museums.* Washington: Smithsonian Institution, Conservation Analytical Lab, 1985. 165 p.

Explains how to identify many common pests, describes their potential to cause damage to a collection, and outlines a variety of controlling strategies. Especially strong on non-chemical management approaches. Extensive bibliography.

Smithsonian Institution, Conservation Analytical Lab, Washington, DC 20560. Free.

Thomson, Garry. *The Museum Environment*. 2nd ed. London: Butterworths, 1986. 308 p.

Thorough discussion of damaging effects of light, humidity, and air pollution (with secondary attention to temperature), with recommendations on how to minimize damage. Essential reading, from which many others on this subject are derivative.

Butterworths, Attn: Order Processing, 80 Montvale Ave., Stoneham, MA 02180 (617-438-8464). $39.95.

Walker, Gay, and others. "The Yale Survey: A Large-Scale Survey of Book Deterioration in the Yale University Library." *College & Research Libraries* 46: 111-32 (March 1985).

A comprehensive picture of the physical characteristics and aging of a large research collection. Conclusions also useful in understanding the scope of deterioration of books and paper.

SEE ALSO: I. *Slow Fires*

III. REPAIR & CONSERVATION TREATMENTS

Greenfield, Jane. *Books: Their Care & Repair*. New York: H. W. Wilson, 1983. 204 p.

Useful and practical manual covering a wide variety of simple repairs, with guidance on setting up and equipping a work station.

H. W. Wilson, 950 University Ave., Bronx, NY 10452 (800-367-6770). $30.

Kyle, Hedi. *Library Materials Preservation Manual: Practical Methods for Preserving Books, Pamphlets and Other Printed Materials*. Bronxville, NY: Nicholas T. Smith, 1983. 160 p.

Includes procedures for several book and flat-paper repairs, pamphlet binding, and protective enclosures, with some guidance on establishing a repair unit. Some of the procedures are complex and should be used only after mastering the basic skills and philosophy of conservation.

New York Botanical Garden, Scientific Publications Dept., Bronx, NY 10458 (212-220-8721). $22.50, plus $2.75 shipping.

Milevski, Robert J. *Book Repair Manual*. Carbondale, IL: Illinois Cooperative Conservation Program, 1984. 71 p.

Explains book structure and causes of problems; then offers clear, detailed, and well illustrated procedures for simple repair of hardbacks and adhesive bindings.

Preservation Office, Illinois State Library, 228 Centennial Bldg., Springfield, IL 62756. $5. Prepayment preferred.

Morrow, Carolyn Clark, and Carole Dyal. *Conservation Treatment Procedures: A Manual of Step-by-Step Procedures for the Maintenance and Repair of Library Materials.* 2nd ed. Littleton, CO: Libraries Unlimited, 1986. 200 p.

Describes practical techniques with clear instructions for simple repairs, collection maintenance, and protective enclosures. Discusses assessment of treatment options and establishment of a conservation unit.

Libraries Unlimited, P. O. Box 263, Littleton, CO 80160. $30.

Morrow, Carolyn Clark, and Roy Weinstock, eds. *Library Preservation: Fundamental Techniques.* Washington: Library of Congress, 1986.

A set of six videotapes intended to supplement training by qualified instructors teaching basic conservation procedures for general collections materials. In each, a leading authority in conservation explains how to apply each procedure, then provides a detailed demonstration of the technique. Tapes in the series, with their instructors and lengths, are: "Books in General Collections: Recasing" (Don Etherington, 79 min.); "Books in General Collections: Paper Repair and Pockets" (Robert Milevski, 81 mins.); "Pamphlet Binding" (Jan Merrill-Oldham, 60 mins.); "Protective Enclosures: Portfolios and Boxes" (Robert Espinosa, 114 mins.); "Protective Enclosures: Simple Wrappers" (Lynn Jones, 52 mins.); and "Protective Enclosures: Surface Cleaning & Encapsulation" (Judith Fortson-Jones, 80 mins.). Supplementary handouts and instructional materials accompany each tape.

LC Information Office, Box A, Washington, DC 20540. $150 for the set in VHS, $375 for 3/4" format. Contact the Office for pricing of individual tapes. Rentals also available; contact the LC National Preservation Program Office (202-287-1840) for information on these.

Ontario Museum Association, and Toronto Area Archivists Group. *Museum & Archival Supply Handbook.* 3rd ed. Toronto: Ontario Museum Assn. and Toronto Area Archivists Group, 1986. 174 p.

Lists over 600 North American suppliers of conservation and archival materials, with some remarks on applications. About 15% of sources in the U.S.

AASLH, 172 Second Ave. North, Suite 102, Nashville, TN 37201 (615-255-2971). $22.25, $19.95 to members. Prepayment required.

Roberts, Matt T., and Don Etherington. *Bookbinding and the Conservation of Books: A Dictionary of Descriptive Terminology.* Washington, DC: Preservation Office, Library of Congress, 1982. 296 p.

A glossary of conservation and bookbinding terms. Helpful to rare books curators, as well as to conservators, binders, and preservation specialists.

S/N 030-000-00126-5. Superintendent of Documents, U. S. Government Printing Office, Washington, DC 20402-9325 (202-783-3238). $27. Prepayment required.

Smith, Merrily A., comp. *Matting and Hinging of Works of Art on Paper*. Washington, DC: Library of Congress, 1981. 32 p.

Practical manual on the appropriate preservation techniques for these procedures.

S/N 030-000-00134-6. Superintendent of Documents, U. S. Government Printing Office, Washington, DC 20402-9325 (202-783-3238). $4.75. Prepayment required.

SEE ALSO: I. Ritzenthaler; VIII. Columbia University Libraries

---

IV. LIBRARY BINDING

NOTE: Perhaps because of the rapid changes occurring in this sphere of preservation, few useful book-length works yet exist, and most up-to-date writings are to be found in journals.

Lanier, Don. *Binding Operations in ARL Libraries*. SPEC Kit 114. Washington: ARL Office of Management Studies, 1985. 105 p.

Includes information from 18 research libraries on organization, operations, staffing, standards and guidelines, and automation in library binding programs.

ARL/OMS, 1527 New Hampshire Ave. NW, Washington, DC 20036 (202-232-8656). $20, $10 members. Prepayment required.

Library Binding Institute. *Library Binding Institute Standard for Library Binding*. 8th ed. Paul A. Parisi and Jan Merrill-Oldham, eds. Rochester: Library Binding Institute, 1986. 17 p.

New edition, extensively revised for the purpose of making library bindings more appropriate as a preservation strategy. Includes specifications for procedures and materials to be used in library binding. Essential reading.

Library Binding Institute, 150 Allens Creek Road, Rochester, NY 14618 (716-461-4380). $5.

Merrill-Oldham, Jan. "Binding for Research Libraries," *New Library Scene* 3: 1, 4-6 (Aug. 1984). Also reproduced in Darling and Boomgaarden (cited in section I).

Outlines a rational decision-making strategy for choosing the appropriate leaf attachment method, and identifies advantages and limitations of each. See follow-up in the August 1985 issue.

"State of Connecticut Binding Contract as Applied to the University of Connecticut Libraries at Storrs." In *Preservation Planning Program: Resource Notebook*, expanded 1987 edition, compiled by Pamela W. Darling and Wesley Boomgaarden, pp. 589-601. Washington: ARL Office of Management Studies, 1987.

An excellent model contract.

Address same as Darling and Boomgaarden (see section I).

Walker, Gay. "Library Binding as a Conservation Measure," *Collection Management* 4: 55-71 (Spring/Summer 1982). Also reproduced in Darling and Boomgaarden (cited in section I).

> Outlines the criteria by which library binding may be considered a "conservation" treatment. Focuses on openability, retention of margins, and longevity.

SEE ALSO: VIII. Columbia University Libraries

V. PRESERVATION MICROFILMING & COPYING

No attempt is made to list the applicable standards and specifications associated with preservation microfilming. Citations for these can be found in the *RLG Preservation Manual* (below) and in catalogues of the American National Standards Institute (1430 Broadway, New York, NY 10018) and the Association for Information and Image Management (1100 Wayne Ave., Silver Spring, MD 20910).

Byrne, Sherry. "Guidelines for Contracting Microfilming Services." *Microform Review* 15: 244-64 (Fall 1986).

> Informative discussion of strategies for using a commercial service bureau in a preservation microfilming program. Includes a helpful model contract.

Council on Library Resources, Commission on Preservation and Access. *Brittle Books: Reports of the Committee on Preservation and Access.* Washington: Council on Library Resources, 1986. 31 p.

> Recommends a national strategy for preserving the informational content of brittle books, especially by microfilming.

> CLR, 1785 Massachusetts Ave. NW, Washington, DC 20036 (202-483-7474). Free.

Gwinn, Nancy E., ed. *Preservation Microfilming: A Guide for Librarians and Archivists.* Chicago: ALA, 1987. 238 p.

> An intelligent, thorough guide to the administrative aspects of planning and operating an institutional preservation microfilming program. Essential reading.

> ALA, 50 East Huron St., Chicago, IL 60611 (800-545-2433). $40.

Kantor, Paul. *Costs of Microfilm Preservation at Research Libraries: A Study of Four Institutions.* Washington: Council on Library Resources, 1986. 32 p.

> Analyzes the costs of each step in a preservation microfilming project (from selection through quality control), and suggests possible means of reducing costs.

> CLR, 1785 Massachusetts Ave. NW, Washington, DC 20036 (202-483-7474). $3. Prepayment required.

McClung, Patricia A. "Costs Associated with Preservation Microfilming: Results of the Research Libraries Group Study." *Library Resources & Technical Services* 30: 363-74 (Oct./Dec. 1986).

Study of the costs associated with preservation microfilming by seven RLG members. Includes both the cash outlay and less direct expenses, such as staff time.

Research Libraries Group. *RLG Preservation Manual.* 2nd ed. Stanford, CA: The Research Libraries Group, 1986. 187 p.

Outlines procedures and specifications for RLG's Cooperative Preservation Microfilming Project, mostly incorporating existing national standards. This has formed the basis for several other preservation microfilming manuals.

RLG Publications Unit, Jordan Quadrangle, Stanford, CA 94305. $14. Prepayment required.

Sung, Carolyn Hoover. *Archives and Manuscripts: Reprography.* SAA Basic Manual Series. Chicago: Society of American Archivists, 1982. 68 p.

A good, practical introduction to reformatting, particularly microfilming of archival records. Covers technical choices, equipment needs, and techniques. Also includes sections on photography and photocopying.

SAA, 600 South Federal, Suite 504, Chicago, IL 60605 (312-922-0140). $8, $6 to members, plus shipping.

Walker, Gay. "Preserving Intellectual Content of Deteriorated Library Materials." In Carolyn Clark Morrow's *The Preservation Challenge: A Guide to Conserving Library Materials*, pp. 93-113. White Plains, NY: Knowledge Industry Publications, 1983.

Excellent overview of the technical options for dealing with brittle books, with discussion of the component procedures in a "brittle books program."

Address same as Morrow (cited in section I).

SEE ALSO: I. Atkinson; I. Child; I. *Slow Fires*; VIII. Office of Management Studies

---

VI. NON-TEXTUAL MATERIALS

Clapp, Anne E. *Curatorial Care of Works of Art on Paper.* 4th ed., revised. New York: Nick Lyons Books, 1987. 191 p.

A clear description of procedures for repair and protection of artworks on paper, intended for the curator and conservation technician. Several sections (e.g., fumigation, relaxation, deacidification) are useful for archive and library conservation labs.

Nick Lyons Books, 31 West 21st St., New York, NY 10010 (212-620-9580). $11.95, plus $1.50 shipping. Prepayment required.

Eastman Kodak Company. *Conservation of Photographs*. Kodak Publication # F-40. Rochester, NY: Eastman Kodak, 1985. 156 p.

Comprehensive guide on preservation and conservation of photographs. Thorough, well organized, clear.

Eastman Kodak, 343 State St., Dept. 454, Rochester, NY 14650. $30.95.

Geller, Sidney B. *Care and Handling of Computer Magnetic Storage Media*. NBS Special Publication 500-101. Washington: National Bureau of Standards, 1983. 128 p.

Detailed manual on care and handling, maintenance, and storage of computer tapes and disks.

S/N 003-003-02486-4. Superintendent of Documents, U. S. Government Printing Office, Washington, DC 20402-9325 (202-703-3238). $5.50. Prepayment required.

McWilliams, Jerry. *The Preservation and Restoration of Sound Recordings*. Nashville: American Association for State and Local History, 1979. 138 p.

A practical, basic guide.

AASLH Order/Billing Dept., 172 Second Ave. North, Suite 102, Nashville, TN 37201 (615-255-2971). $7.75, $6.95 to members. Prepayment required.

Reilly, James M. *Care and Identification of 19th-Century Photographic Prints*. Kodak Publication # G-2S. Rochester, NY: Eastman Kodak, 1986. 116 p.

A detailed description of 19th-century photographic processes, with guidelines for identifying and preserving each.

Image Permanence Institute, RIT City Center, 50 West Main St., Rochester, NY 14614-1274. $24.95, plus $1.50 shipping.

Ritzenthaler, Mary Lynn, Gerald J. Munoff, and Margery S. Long. *Archives & Manuscripts: Administration of Photographic Collections*. SAA Basic Manual Series. Chicago: Society of American Archivists, 1984. 173 p.

Addresses all aspects of managing photographic collections, from appraisal and accession through research and publication. Preservation specifically discussed in one chapter, but pervades the entire book.

SAA, 600 South Federal, Suite 504, Chicago, IL 60605 (312-922-0140). $19, $14 to members, plus shipping.

Swartzburg, Susan G., ed. *Conservation in the Library: A Handbook on Use and Care of Traditional and Nontraditional Materials*. Westport, CT: Greenwood Press, 1983. 234 p.

Essays on the care and handling of a wide range of library materials. Especially useful are the sections on non-book formats, with excellent articles on: photographs, slides, microforms, motion picture film, videotape, sound recordings, and videodiscs.

Greenwood Press, Attn: Order Dept., 88 Post Road West, P. O. Box 5007, Westport, CT 06881 (203-226-3571). $39.95, plus shipping. Prepayment usually required.

SEE ALSO: III. Smith

VII. EMERGENCY PREPAREDNESS

Barton, John P., and Johanna G. Wellheiser, eds. *An Ounce of Prevention: A Handbook on Disaster Contingency Planning for Archives, Libraries and Record Centres*. Toronto: Toronto Area Archivists Group Education Foundation, 1985. 192 p.

> One of the most practical and comprehensive manuals published on disaster prevention, planning, and recovery.

> TAAG, P. O. Box 97, Station F, Toronto, Ontario M4Y 2L4 Canada; $22.95 Canadian. Also available from: SAA, 600 South Federal, Suite 504, Chicago, IL 60605 (312-922-0140); $16, $14 to members, plus shipping. NOTE: This book is reportedly unavailable from TAAG at this time, due to the authors' plans to issue a new edition.

Morris, John. *Managing the Library Fire Risk*. 2nd ed. Berkeley: Univ. of California, 1979. 147 p.

> Clearly explains various fire prevention and extinguishing technologies, and provides case studies of some disastrous library fires.

> John Morris, 3333 Nutmeg Lane, Walnut Creek, CA 94598 (415-933-3365). $15.50.

Murray, Toby, compiler. "Bibliography on Disasters, Disaster Preparedness and Disaster Recovery." Tulsa: Oklahoma Conservation Congress, 1986. 24 p.

> A comprehensive bibliography of bibliographies, books, reports, and articles. Frequently updated.

> Preservation Officer, Oklahoma Department of Libraries, 200 Northeast 18th St., Oklahoma City, OK 73105. Free.

Myers, Gerald E. *Insurance Manual for Libraries*. Chicago: ALA, 1977. 64 p.

> Concise, helpful guide.

> ALA, 50 East Huron St., Chicago, IL 60611 (800-545-2433). Out of print.

Myers, James N., and Denise D. Bedford, eds. *Disasters: Prevention and Coping*. Proceedings of the Conference, May 21-22, 1980. Stanford: Stanford University Libraries, 1981. 177 p.

> Several good papers on a whole range of disaster preparedness topics.

> Stanford University Libraries Publications Office, Stanford, CA 94305 (415-723-9434). $18.

National Fire Protection Association. *NFPA 910: Recommended Practice for the Protection of Libraries and Library Collections; 1985 edition*. Quincy: National Fire Protection Association, 1985. 24 p.

> Information on technology for fire detection and extinguishing systems, with results of tests on the efficacy of compact storage in reducing fire damage. ANSI-approved.

NFPA Publication Sales Division, Batterymarch Park, Quincy, MA 92269 (800-344-3555). $12, plus $2.85 shipping.

New York University Libraries Preservation Committee. *Disaster Plan Workbook*. New York: NYU Libraries, 1984. 75 p.

Essentially a "fill-in-the-blanks" disaster plan, with some basic information on emergency procedures and resources. Should be used in conjunction with more detailed literature on the subject.

Collection Management Office, Bobst Library, NYU, 70 Washington Square South, New York, NY 10012. $10.

Sable, Martin H. *The Protection of the Library and Archive: An International Bibliography*. New York: Haworth Press, 1983. 183 p. Reprinted from *Library & Archival Security* 5 (Summer/Fall 1983).

Extensive bibliography arranged chronologically by subject.

Haworth Press, 12 West 32nd St., New York, NY 10001 (607-722-2493). $29.95, plus $2 shipping.

Waters, Peter. *Procedures for Salvage of Water Damaged Library Materials*. 2nd ed. Washington: Library of Congress, 1979. 30 p.

Policy and procedures to assess damage and to plan and carry out salvage operations, including stabilization and recovery techniques. This edition is out of date in many ways, but a 3rd edition is being prepared.

S/N 030-000-00105-2. Superintendent of Documents, U. S. Government Printing Office, Washington, DC 20402-9325 (202-703-3238). Out of print.

Zeidberg, David S. *Collection Security in ARL Libraries*. SPEC Kit 100. Washington: ARL Office of Management Studies, 1985. 94 p.

Includes policy statements, procedural documents, and task force reports from selected research libraries.

ARL/OMS, 1527 New Hampshire Ave. NW, Washington, DC 20036 (202-232-8656). $20, $10 members. Prepayment required.

VIII. PROGRAM PLANNING & ADMINISTRATION

Calmes, Alan, Ralph Schofer, and Keith R. Eberhardt. *National Archives and Records Service (NARS) Twenty Year Preservation Plan*. NBSIR 85-2999. Gaithersburg, MD: National Bureau of Standards, 1985. 67 p.

Reports on an extensive collection condition survey and the resulting comprehensive preservation plan developed for the National Archives.

National Technical Information Service, U. S. Dept. of Commerce, 5285 Port Royal Rd., Springfield, VA 22161. $10.

Columbia University Libraries Preservation Department. *The Preservation of Library Materials: A CUL Handbook.* 4th ed. New York: Columbia University Libraries, 1987.

Detailed guidelines for CUL staff on library binding, repair, replacement, microfilming, collection maintenance, and disaster preparedness. A useful model.

Gifts & Exchange Dept., 104 Butler Library, 535 W. 114th St., Columbia University, New York, NY 10027 (212-280-3532). $15.

Darling, Pamela W., with Duane E. Webster. *Preservation Planning Program: An Assisted Self-Study Manual for Libraries.* Expanded 1987 ed. Washington: ARL Office of Management Studies, 1987. Approx. 147 p.

Developed to help libraries plan and implement preservation programs in a process that educates and involves a large number of staff members. Outlines a self-study process for assessing needs, setting priorities, and planning a program. Involves planning modules on: environmental conditions, physical condition of the collection, organization and staffing, disaster control, education of staff and users, and inter-institutional cooperation. Augmented by Darling and Boomgaarden's *Resource Notebook* (cited in section I). Final reports of institutions that have completed the formal self-study are also available from OMS.

ARL/OMS, 1527 New Hampshire Ave. NW, Washington, DC 20036 (202-232-8656). $15. Prepayment required.

Godden, Irene P., and Myra Jo Moon. *Organizing for Preservation in ARL Libraries.* SPEC Kit 116. Washington: ARL Office of Management Studies, 1985. 131 p.

Documents from 15 research libraries with active preservation programs; includes organizational charts, position descriptions, required qualifications, background information on program development.

ARL/OMS, 1527 New Hampshire Ave. NW, Washington, DC 20036 (202-232-8656). $20, $10 to members. Prepayment required.

Merrill-Oldham, Jan. *Preservation Education in ARL Libraries.* SPEC Kit 113. Washington: ARL Office of Management Studies, 1985. 110 p.

Describes ways to increase preservation awareness of staff members, patrons, and other constituents. Includes a wealth of sample materials used by selected ARL libraries.

ARL/OMS, 1527 New Hampshire Ave. NW, Washington, DC 20036 (202-232-8656). $20, $10 to members. Prepayment required.

Merrill-Oldham, Jan, and Merrily Smith, eds. *The Library Preservation Program: Models, Priorities, Possibilities.* Chicago: ALA, 1985. 117 p.

Seventeen excellent papers address the history and importance of preservation, offer administrative models, discuss organization of a preservation program in relation to institutional priorities and available options, and address the fiscal realities. An outstanding publication.

ALA, 50 E. Huron, Chicago, IL 60611 (800-545-2433). $8.95.

National Research Council, Committee on Preservation of Historical Records. *Preservation of Historical Records*. Washington: National Academy Press, 1986. 108 p.

Detailed report on a study of the condition of materials and preservation needs at the National Archives. Useful information on the effects of the environment, types of paper deterioration, and treatment and reformatting options.

National Academy Press, 2101 Constitution Ave. NW, Washington, DC 20418. $17.95.

Office of Management Studies, ARL. *Preservation Guidelines for ARL Libraries*. SPEC Kit 137. Washington: ARL Office of Management Studies, 1987. 110 p.

Reproduces documents from 16 research libraries with active preservation programs; includes preservation policy documents, priority statements, documents related to decision-making, and descriptions of brittle books programs.

ARL/OMS, 1527 New Hampshire Ave. NW, Washington, DC 20036 (202-232-8656). $20, $10 to members. Prepayment required.

IX. SERIAL PUBLICATIONS

The Abbey Newsletter. Bimonthly.

Excellent source of timely information on preservation and conservation subjects, including bookbinding, commercial binding, educational programs, publications, supply sources, and news. Essential reading for the full-time preservation specialist.

Ellen McCrady, editor; 300 East Center, Provo, UT 84601. $35/year.

CAN: Conservation Administration News. Quarterly.

Focuses on preservation administration, with accounts of program development, announcements of workshops, reviews of publications, conference reports.

Robert Patterson, editor; McFarlin Library, Univ. of Tulsa, 600 South College Ave., Tulsa, OK 74104. $18/year.

International Preservation News. Occasional.

Produced by the IFLA Core Programme on Preservation & Conservation (PAC). Reports on preservation activities of IFLA; highlights international activities and events that support efforts to preserve the materials in the world's libraries and archives.

Merrily Smith, editor; IFLA PAC; c/o National Preservation Program Office, LM-G07, Library of Congress, Washington, DC 20540. Free to interested institutions.

Microform Review. Five issues per year.

Contains articles on microform librarianship and, increasingly, preservation microfilming.

Meckler Publishing, 11 Ferry Lane West, Westport, CT 06880 (203-226-6967). $115/year.

National Preservation News. Quarterly.

Produced by the National Preservation Program Office, Library of Congress. Highlights national and other cooperative preservation efforts within the U.S. and abroad, and reports on preservation activities at LC.

National Preservation Program Office, LM-G07, Library of Congress, Washington, DC 20540. Free to interested institutions.

New Library Scene. Bimonthly.

Excellent information on library binding services and trends, with increasing emphasis on the relationship between binding and other preservation concerns.

Library Binding Institute, 150 Allens Creek Road, Rochester, NY 14618. $18/year.

Technology & Conservation. Quarterly.

Reports on current programs and projects, with focus on technical aspects of conservation of art, architecture, and antiquities.

The Technology Organization, 1 Emerson Place, Boston, MA 02114. Free to "qualified practitioners," $12/year to others.

239045